HUGH McMILLAN is a poet from⌐   He
has written five full collections o   try
festivals worldwide. His pamphle   of
the Callum Macdonald Prize in 2   *ed*
in 2017; as part of that prize, he became Michael Marks Poet in Residence
for the Harvard Summer School in Napflio, Greece. He was also a winner
of the Smith Doorstep Poetry Prize and the Cardiff International Poetry
Competition. *Devorgilla's Bridge* was shortlisted for the Michael Marks
Award and in 2015 was shortlisted for the Basil Bunting Poetry Award. In
2014 Hugh was awarded the first literature commission by the Wigtown
Book Festival to create a work inspired by John Mactaggart's *The Scottish
Gallovidian Encyclopaedia* (1824); *McMillan's Galloway* was published in
limited edition in 2014 and in a revised edition from Luath in 2015.

His selected poems Not Actually Being in Dumfries were published by Luath
Press in 2015 and this was followed by Heliopolis and The Conversation of
Sheep by Luath in 2018.

He has featured in many anthologies, and three times in the Scottish Poetry
Library's online selection Best Scottish Poems of the year. His poems have
also been chosen three times to feature on National Poetry Day postcards,
the latest in 2016. In 2020 he was chosen as one of four 'Poetry Champions'
for Scotland by the Scottish Poetry Library, to seek out and commission
new work. Recently he was given the role as editor of 'Best Scottish Poems'
for 2021."

By the same author:

Tramontana, Dog and Bone, 1990
Horridge, Chapman, 1995
Aphrodite's Anorak, Peterloo Poets, 1996
Strange Bamboo, Shoestring, 2007
Postcards from the Hedge, Roncadora Press, 2009
Devorgilla's Bridge, Roncadora Press, 2010
Cairn, Roncadora Press, 2011
Thin Slice of Moon, Roncadora Press, 2012
McMillan's Galloway, privately printed, 2015
Not Actually being in Dumfries, Luath Press, 2015
McMillan's Galloway: A Creative Guide by an Unreliable Local, Luath Press, 2017
Sheepenned, Roncadora Press, 2017
Heliopolis, Luath Press, 2018
The Conversation of Sheep, Luath Press, 2018
Whit If?, Luath Press, 2021

Haphazardly in the Starless Night

HUGH McMILLAN

Luath Press Limited
EDINBURGH
www.luath.co.uk

First published 2021

ISBN: 978-1-910022-89-4

The paper used in this book is recyclable. It is made from low chlorine pulps produced in a low energy, low emission manner from renewable forests.

Printed and bound by Severn, Gloucester

Typeset in 10.5 point Sabon by Lapiz

Contents

PORTENTS

7

Wraiths

The Nature of Art

Art was always a thing in our house
or artiness: we were thought of
as bohemians,

had the qualifications:
poverty, scandal, a frisson of madness.
My father, stuck in rage and guilt,

wrote a short story about a soldier
in a desert stuck in rage and guilt
and painted birds that could not fly.

My sister drew a landscape
she walked into.
I wrote a poem about snow

that never fell, filled gaps like that
with empty words.
My mother tore a photograph

of the MV *Columba* from a brochure
or the *People's Friend*,
stuck it on the wall

with sellotape that yellowed
as the years passed,
wished she was there.

The Wishbone

On the windowsill,
its white paint old
and flaking,
was a wishbone,

a pewter pot beside it
that my mother said
was from home.
Moss mould was

on the edges of glass
and on the outside
the perpetual dark
of weeds gone wild.

There was a wishbone
on the windowsill,
it was huge like a dinosaur's,
yellow and stained

with the ghost of blood.
A pterodactyl bone,
a pagan bone,
the fundament of a roc.

It was there for years
while round it the house
fell apart. It's still there
in a shelf of my mind.

No one did.
No one dared really.

My Father at the Bakers

On the veranda
is a bony old man
who but for
the kombolói
reminds me
of my father.
He has a thin
moustache
and baggy shorts
and his right
foot is agitating
at the marble
as if

pumping some
accelerator
that would have
him in a wish
at the top
of that mountain
concealed now
in cloud
and haze.
If he were here
I would ask him
if he preferred
mountains

to coastlines,
you are supposed
to be one
or the other
I would say.

So many questions
and still
a language barrier.
It's a fantasy
thinking of him
like this,
I can't have seen
him old.

Perhaps
in my mind
he has
aged with me
though this too
is a fruitless
train of thought
because one
of the few facts
I know
is that he's
dust.
We'll just sit here

for a moment
his doppelgänger
and I
and stare
at a middle
distance
populated
this hot
and sultry
morning
by the living
the imagined
and the dead.

The Wait

Kippers catapult me back
to Victorian hotels with huge
rain-slashed vistas,
brittle toast and butter knobs,
sugar lumps like granite,
paintings of mouldering birds
on thick wallpaper.

I remember every kipper
but not so much the people,
though they certainly comprised
a bald man in a sports jacket,
decrepit car rusting outside,
and his wife, whose homeland
was hidden, like her,

in sad cloud
beyond the bay windows.
What did we even do
except order kippers
and stare silently at the sea?
I suppose we were waiting always
for the weather to clear.

Benches of Wigtown

A new bench is here today
in full throated sunshine
that turns silt channels
into unearthly lanes of light.
This is an ancient site
and graves and harbours
lie under shifting moss
picked over by ragged sheep
and shrill swooping birds.
'Rest your Butt' it advises

on a plaque, where the names
of the dead jostle with those
who clubbed together to buy
the seat. It is wide enough
to rest all their butts

as they sit for a few years
to recall the clever dead,
the brash living.
At a few hundred paces
either way older benches

are swallowed in ivy
and wild rose, they are melting
into the language of landscape
where all signals and memories go,
where all butts are restless bone.

George Catlin and the Moon–Eyes

The Moon-Eyes shunned the sun,
too pale, too small, too bearded.
Catlin thought them Welsh,
washed up in Tennessee
after a wrong turn years before.

The Cherokee made light work of them,
chased them off to roles
in the civil service and light opera.
Catlin loved his moon–eyed Indians
and painted them for the Blaze Channel

where in years to come
they would prove that once
upon a time ancient aliens
came here to teach us about
the innate energy in limestone

and stick implants in our
heads, implants which SOME SAY
race lost star maps from our DNA.
Catlin was full of moon dust:
bankrupt and half daft

he painted his Indians through thick
and thin, in person, from memory,
from the depths of imagination,
his record of a dying race.
Some say his passion was prompted

by a secret family in the Mandan,
his own moon kids and moon wife
in the lush forest
pale and lovely and lost always,
except at the end of a brush.

Glayva

I am drinking a Glayva
in search of my mother
who drank occasionally,
not like a highlander at all,

that or port and lemon.
They are elusive her lot,
photo shy, not even buried
where they're meant to be,

the odd picture of a cottage,
collie dog, honeysuckle.
It's like they were planning
all along to go to earth.

After their tidy – or untidy,
who can tell – lives as
fishermen, postmistresses,
ladies maids, and labourers,

they melted into the warm
landscape like rain into soil.
And only a taste, a douce
spirit is left on the tongue.

The Cart Track

There's a photograph
of children balancing
on the bales
on their way back

from that lost school
in the glen
They are in half tilt
down the hill

the road rutted even then
one lassie is just clinging
on but not caring
she's in mid laugh

Behind her the river
winds wider than now
there are stooks
in the fields dots

that may be people
making a last mark
on a century
of black and white

Walk the track now
it has narrowed
like arteries
room between

the rhododendrons
for a Saturday stroll

with a fat Labrador
a view through the trees

to the village
strung down there
its bright empty houses
pink lemon white

Autumn in Scotland

The dogs are barking
to distant dogs
whose voices are on the edge
of hearing.
How many dogs are barking
silhouetted on the rusting sides
of tractors,
by streams slowly bearing
dead leaves,
by cold floors
and fireplaces tonight?
Through the hills
and woods
through the colours
of our mothers and fathers,
all their tears even,
through this land, this land,
the dogs are barking.

The Language of the Sun

Dreams are real,
the sun is an infection.
I appear near the end
of the book I am reading,

suave plot resolver,
nemesis, town drunk,
blazing, sun bubbling
through my veins

like paint stripper.
I peel. I am wiped out.
Green is the colour
of my gardens and

silence the roar
of the Earth turning.
Ghosts stand by rough
cast walls and old azaleas.

In the language
of the sun we are all one,
the living, the dead,
the dreamers.

It Was That Time of Night, John

I've often wondered at night
when I listen for the wind
is it the time the body says that's it,
good point to finish, the dawn
just a hem between trees
and the birds beginning to stir?

We go to bed in our little
houses, having wiped the kitchen
table clean, patted the cats,
pursed dry lips at the rain,
then pad up to bed hoping
to wake no one in the passing.

A Picture of the Vessel *Agnes*, Near Dockfoot

Taken here most likely,
at this mooring now
swamped by grass
and fired by columbine.

The barque is sleek,
bowspritted and carvel built,
reeking I think
of fresh logs and linseed,

her figurehead carved
with the face of the owner's
daughter, a beauty
dead of smallpox.

Her arm is raised,
palm upwards, to soothe
the angry seas.
The crew must be

at the Mermaid or the
Turk's Head, brandy alive
in their blood. It is a hot day
I think, the town

in early summer heat haze.
Some figures on the bank
merge with the glare like ghosts.
I strain my eyes, look further

beyond the blur
where photograph leaks
to history and shimmers
like mercury.

Only imagination
crosses the river there
and it is easy through the filter
of a little reading
and some episodes

of *Poldark* to feel Dumfries
rollicking with dark life and love.
I know one thing, though,

from the immutability of records.
The ship will slip out soon
on a full tide
and never return.

The Trip up North I Never Went on with Tim Propp

I Never Went on with Tim Propp

We started in the Kelvin –
no Wetherspoons, too
impersonal –

then went to Auleys Bar,
the Tartan Lounge
and Markie Dans

then back
to take in the ones we missed.
The small pubs were

best because he filled them.
In each, the barmaid
knew his name and as he came in,

a small crowd hurried
to greet him. They were all folk
who had a yearning,

a kind of sadness
or story to tell, and who
were illuminated by him,

the size, the accent,
the time he had for every
one of them.

At some point
we discussed the things
we always meant to,
which I think were to do
with wayward romanticism
and lost causes.

I don't remember
really:
I must have gone to lie down

after chips and a double something
but when I looked out the window
it was unmistakably him,

shouldering his bag
along the long promenade,
on his way.

Ring of Water

The ring of water
is here under covert cloud,
behind the wake of a steamer.
Through a collar of rain
the little moon picks it out.

It's no Corryvreckan.
Some say it is
splintered lamplight
from the circus of shorelines
but they are wrong,

it is a fairy tide circling:
it is little arteries
of dark light and bubble
like blood
and every pantomime

and tragedy we have
has been enacted here
in its shadows,
in the circling
of its arms, however time

and geography
suggest otherwise.
There is no logic
to the little ring of light,
it is God and Mother

and love and the nearness
of death.

Hoard

In laboratories they will
piece together
the flakes of centuries
tightly bound in silk and wool

and make
maps
and caravans and
long dead journeys,

but the balls of dirt,
and black stone
with its dull heart,
no carbon dating

will unveil their meaning,
no scalpel unpeel
a script or scroll:
I can tell you about these.

I found one by the Scaur,
have seen them borne
home by my kids,
these are talismans

more precious than
their equivalent in gold,
they are weights,
measurements

of unwritten stories,
buried in the heart
for a single span.

The Poet

When asked, the poet could not
remember the names of her books,
in fact could not remember there
were any books at all, but sat down
and hand-wrote from memory on

tight foolscap seven poems,
including one several pages long.
You see she explained, you see,
dear dear man, my memory
is not so good and I have been

called frail but it's strange that
when I recall those days in
Muirkirk which means the church
on the moor, I see things quite
clearly, and these poems which

I am sending you are like that:
winter scenes and stirks and auld
fowk and wee lassies – I wrote
about them in the language of the
people. And here they are now, always.

Going

I'm going for a flu jag
past the small stunted trees
of Thornhill which are waiting
patiently for another year.
It is in their make-up

this grave attendance,
and even when the flowers
come they are counting
the days till they fall
though not rancorously,

there is no regret in
the arithmetic, simply
holy truth. When we fall
there is no such dignity.
I have often dreamed

of standing on the shores
of Loch Maree, the mountains
slowly warming in light,
the unfathomable water,
the islands beaded

with silent stones.
The best views have
no people but they are
always at the edge,
infecting scenes

with their longing.
They have left in ships
or books or poems.
They are always leaving,
when wanting most to stay.

The Alexandria Quartet

Fifty years since we bought the book,
mooching one Saturday
among the kiosks and bordellos
on the west bank of the Nith,

and shared it: our names
bracketed on the fly leaf.
From the very beginning –
my mind's eye shows me

a thousand tormented streets –
we wanted to be in Alexandria
or at least an imitation,
somewhere with dwarves,

and Melissa and Justine
to be torn languidly between.
We were ok for dwarves,
but in every other respect

Dumfries with its damp mist
and bonneted old men
didn't fit the bill, it was
too hard to imagine

doing battle with the tireless
apathy of the summer air.
The tireless apathy of the summer air,
page 96, that's where I ended,

the perfect place that September,
a line made for me.

He was different, more dogged.
For weeks we'd swopped

but then our lives diverged.
It was his turn, he forgot,
I was away from home, there were
other schemes and friends,

we lost touch, he got ill,
and who cares about an unread book?
But when he died it came back.
I have it now, in my hands,

and the touch brings
a mix of loss and wasted time.
Page 96, still dog-eared,
but there are others further on,

like footholds in a climb.
Perhaps like Malory he'd made it
and perished coming down,
white faced and quiet,

through half lit paragraphs
to where it all began,
with the shadow light of evening,
the rapture of return.

Twelve Roads

1

Thin ribbons of water
like spokes of a wheel,
lambs insouciant at fence posts,
moors where shabby cows
hawk out pats.
Land of the conventicle,
the sour opinion sourly given:
the sky is oatmeal here,
the colour of porridge,
but half an hour ago the treetops
were electric green.
This bit of country needs
the sun –
needs a face on

2

Three kids skiving school,
swinging through thin
white Scottish trees,
trees that have done some
heavy smoking by the
railway line, hard
paper-round trees,
trees that arenae deid
yet, thirty years old but
look sixty. Kids not going
quietly, looming
through the ghostly
paperbarks banging metal plates
like Kelly's gang:
come and get us, copper

3

Rails thicken like arteries
and bushes bud plastic,
black soil detritus –
an explosion
of people is coming
glorious but deadly,
blessed and cursed,
their hive is irresistible.
How many hours, days,
weeks spent here
meeting myself in pub-light,
in the mirrors of grim toilets,
cheery wave –
I used to say Shug how
are you doing, because
honestly I didn't know

4

North grey waters
hulks and
flotsam. This water is scarred,
rainbowed by oil,
pocked by jetties
like dead teeth.
Tobacco ships and blood money,
now floating bombs like black slugs.
The hillsides tumoured with bunkers.
A primary school on top
perched like a ripe cherry.
Green eco flag.
No sense of irony, the birch twists away
at an angle
as though imagining
the unimaginable

5

Islands seal shaped
in silver light piercing
cloud like needles:
what light what light
on a horizon so endless.
Cowled water birds,
the inlets outlets
in mercury to the lips of the world.
When has a shore been so cruel
and a horizon so inviting?

6

Chip shop doorway.
In the cathedral of the
world we still have
to eat, in the drizzle of the holy,
in the lap of the everyday.
In our lonely dargs
we live and the landscape
laughs and shrugs
but at least it says something

7

Truly we have travelled
beyond railways now,
man has run out of steam,
poetry is inculcated in
the map:
Suilven, Cùl Mòr, Foinaven.
Ben More Assynt

If you believe in Gods
they are here watching.
squatting with
ugly square faces
and warts as we employ
the might of our
two-hundredweight fleece
and Gore-Tex
against elemental truth
and come away with
nothing but flim flam,
that poor exchange
for living, memories.
Best to stand
and scream
and not articulate it
as rage or longing or misery
but simply and purely as scream.
You'll not be the last

8

The inclination to keep going
till you drop off the end.
How many lost this year,
last year. Lunacy moves north
who said that? One of the lost.
It's the brilliance though,
a jewel path to the Arctic North
where every feeling freezes.
A newspaper says a golden age
is coming, the north
west passage is melting.
Scotland will become the hub

of a network from Vladivostok
to Nova Scotia. Our ships
will ply ghost routes
with ghost cargoes.
There were golden ages here
though, the stones speak
of it, when we were part
of nature, not set above it
like some fin de siecle frilly bunnet,
some sad end of supper joke

9

The slate road, the fish road,
the fish supper road,
nuggets of harbours,
camper vans choking
postcard views.
A smaller sea but vicious.
I remember mad fathers
and tin caravan
roofs, rain drumming
like a soldier's funeral,
lightning far off across water.
My journey, my family's,
like nomads circling
this squat, lovely tortured land,
till gravity and the plug hole got us

10

The great grey toun – I am at home here
in its cosy darknesses,
in its wreck of anecdote.
Its anecdotage I should say for here

is the place to namedrop.
It is where to come to die
with a pint of posh lager
and easy access to the emergency
services. It is the home of poetry
and politics, dubious practices
that generally attract vain fools.
Some angels lived here
but watch, I am opening
my mind like a seedy film house
specialising in cult classics.
I am not looking for old film but for the pure
unencumbered word

11

Where is love
in all this I hear the question
It is there, the words in the poem,
the words in the song,
the text on the screen,
it is a subtitle to all this
and the best way of seeing it.
Not the only way,
and not the longest lasting –
it will not see out
glaciation or furnace –
but the best,
so now under smooth hills
unnaturally green,
a glass raised to love,
which of course is hope

12

From the egg to the apple.
Home is where the Airbnb is,
the splintered grouse,
the easy cringe.
We lie beneath Gaelic names
but grunt when we speak
at all. An empty place.
But the paths walked
by our children will be
sacred forever, or at least for
the moment we have to think
and remember. They will
be the last things we do,
seeking to look
through the child's eye
before the world was spoiled.
Full circle

At Sea

I'm having scallops
and Sauvignon Blanc
in a restaurant with huge
windows and the sea
and sun are throwing
light on my face.

When I was here
with my mother it was
the Fishermen's Mission.
The walls were painted
dark blue and she had
a long faded coat,

not because she was poor
but because she
is from the past.
Everything is dark blue
in the past and half seen,
the wallpaper, the pictures

with nothing on them,
the faces with nothing
on them, a tea urn maybe.
A giant tea urn,
or no tea urn at all.
The mind has one go

and the past is stuck there
rinsed by other stuff,
old films, other photos,
you or others thinking

it can't have been
like that, probably

more like this.
At the end what's left
is that colour, dark blue,
and my mother saying
this is nice, they help
people lost at sea.

The Queen of Bohemia's Allegorical Garden

Elizabeth Stuart's garden
at Heidelberg was wondrous.
Dug from the side
of a mountain it was

a boast in cold stone,
a masonic Alhambra,
every terrace and loggia
cunningly engineered.

Neptune was out-Neptuned,
Mars wore the Imperial crown.
In mazes lined by marble,
logicians wandered lost,

for poets there were
grottos with canals
and gilded swans,
for scientists, automata

in trees charmed like birds
of the Americas,
and for philosophers,
Urania presided over all

with a golden rod
that acted as a sundial,
the shadow of time
moving inexorably across

the carefully sculpted
landscape, the orange trees
blazing all the while
in the sunlight like flags.

When Spring came,
armies gathered like clouds
from everywhere,
as if called.

Marguerite D'Écosse

Margaret Stewart
wrote poetry every evening.
She was loved for it by a few
but to most of the courtiers
she was the butt of jokes:

they laughed at her clothes,
her diet, her manners,
but most of all her desire
to write: as if a teenager
from the savage north could

have noble fancies and
the skill and wit to pen them.
Her husband hated her,
married her for her dowry
of Scottish troops,

tore her verses up when she
died. He was a successful King:
in other words a brutal thug
with libraries of books
written about him,

but she is remembered
in the vague and beautiful
ways that matter to some,
in scraps and stories
that might be dreams.

They say the master writer
Alain Chartier,
France's finest, had a vision
where she graced him
with a poet's kiss.

The Museum of Memory

The Museum of Memory
in Chatila
is little more than a shack
that reeks of oil
and cigarette smoke.
It holds old pots and pans,
faded papers, documents,
other tat.

There are no videos
or interactive panels.
No curator
much of the time,
but people wander in
and out to smell
or touch or sit
in the mess of the past.

History is not much
more than a joke,
the ghosts
of men and maps,
but memories
are something else,
especially the memories
that are not our own.

Kamel holds
his grandfather's key,
huge, made from solid iron,
the key to a locked door
of a locked house,

a farm left in haste
a blur of years ago
and all these things

are dust now,
the walls gone,
the furniture broken,
the trees torn down,
all lost beyond the key only,
which Kamel turns
over and over in his palm
and unlocks air.

Christmas at the Hair Boutique the Day after the Election that Plunged Britain into Gloom

Aye dinnae laugh am gan
oan a cage fightin trip tae Ireland:
I follaw the cage fightin
or boaxin, onything whaur folk

get battert, ma ma says
Laura yir a sadist but it's a laugh
ken naebody gets hurt really,
never been tae Dublin but

it'll be different fae Sanquhar,
last Christmas we aa went
tae Portpatrick in a log cabin
can ye imagine bit poash fur me,

this year wir gan
tae Benidorm apart frae gran
she disnae like tae fly,
dye want it cut ower yer ears?

Last time we wir oan a plane
there wis an Elvis
impersonator he was steamin
drunk had tae be removed

felt sorry fur his boy
but ma dad got a laugh
whaun he said Elvis has left
the boeing. Life's aye

hard but ye've goat tae look
on the bright side.
There, ye'll feel a bit
lighter noo.

Scottish Poet Killed while Trying to say the Right Thing about Burns

The first fatality
of Burns Night was recorded
this morning when a poet
struggling to make a tribute to the Bard
fell into a well-known paradox.

Mathew Wingnut, 46,
a poet living near Cumnock,
suffered multiple injuries in the incident.
'It's a tragedy' said a local health professional,
'at this time of year

so many poets are jostling
to say something meaningful
yet modern about Burns
that accidents inevitably happen.'
Mr Wingnut is thought to have

been making an elaborate case
for Burns to be judged
in the context of his
times when he became dizzy
and fell into the abyss.

'It was an incredibly difficult
manoeuvre for him to be attempting
at that stage of his career,
and in these conditions'
said an expert.

Mr Wingnut's local writing group
led tributes to the wordsmith
and Rab Gordon, Nith Valley
Makar, was reported as
'feelin unco thrawn'.

SALE

Today I must turn a penny for my work.
There are things to sort out:
my girls must travel
beyond the rain and rage
to see the the sun turn
a million pebbles into fire.

So I have a poem
about trees: there is plenty imagery
in it, you might say it is bursting
with muscle. And I am
particularly pleased with this one
about the sea – it's been

on a shelf for some time
pulsating weirdly. It has fish.
Then there is a box of family ones –
upset them and watch the words
spill brawling across the floor!
I will take them out on the street

and put them on a small
fold-up table marked POEMS
and tell passers-by
what they cost in time
that could have been spent
less painfully. I will have

a hand-written note that says
NO CARDS or CHEQUES
but I will let the poems go for what
they're worth: a moment's reading:
the time taken
for your life to touch mine.

Portents

Jasmine at a Maths Exam

Jasmine is looking at the wall
where there are three clocks
marking the same ponderous
passage of time from noon

till one, via every station
of the cross. There is more chance
of her shifting the hands
by telekinesis than calculating

the area of that regular pentagon,
or the depth (d) of water
in that guttering, or giving answer 3c
as a surd. There is the sigh

of wind and a large glass panel,
beyond which trees bend
and a river named after
a Goddess moves forever

to the sea. Teachers
will say these things
are maths but some people
aren't happy until they

reduce every miracle
to a box they can take home
and tick. What I'm calculating here –
in the eyes, the head bent

behind the corkscrews
of dark hair she's twisting –
is the torque of love,
the vectors of wasted time.

Lydia Just Before her Life Changes

Lydia is sitting
with her profile against
the bay at Halikoura.
The headland is
wreathed in light cloud,
and it is the beginning
of night.
We are feeding cats

from a huge plate
of marida –
small grilled fish –
that I am unable
to finish.
There are a host
of cats under
the skirt of the table:

a tabby, a one-eyed ginger
who may be simple,
others which make
a cameo appearance,
blurring round
the tablecloth
like a fresco.
They are already

fading into history
these cats.
We are in a tavern
off the beaten track,
we are alone
with the sea

and the last burn
of the sun

and the future,
who is like a person
bathing just off shore
before confidently
walking through
the surf
and towelling himself
down.

A Curlew Cries

Through cupped leaves,
sun boomerangs from cloud via
mirrors of slate and dyke.
The broom is like a blaze.

I'm walking with my daughter
and her hair, too, is fire.
It is Sunday in Galloway
so no buses, only miles of grass,

and a brae to cripple you.
We listen to the chorus of birds,
sheep and bees. I pick out the curlew:
it is the sound most like goodbye.

I wonder when a day like this,
so perfect in many verifiable ways,
first became an elegy for every other
day like this? A time of year when

suddenly the colour of light becomes
the same as sadness. She takes my hand,
briefly, she is not a child, and we walk
far into the cloister of the glen.

Burntisland Sept 6th

Young sandpipers
hoovering shallows and
the sun has dipped for a moment
below clouds so the mud
and rocks gently gutter and burn.

The sea is a mile away
polishing rocks
and a molten strip of sand
is lit and ribbons the bay
like a gift which it is,

until the next train at least,
creaks and hoots to Aberdour.
In that time just birds nagging
offshore and a dog asleep
on the sand and a man

in a blue coat
walking back and forth
on the promenade
singing a song under his breath
which I can't quite catch.

Watching Andy Goldsworthy Being Collected in a Taxi

The cutting edge of poetry
or maybe in fact the slightly
corroded bit of a blunt fork,
the tine – that's it I am the blunt

tine of poetry – is onerous:
there are painful bus rides
through parts of Lanarkshire
and buying pints at Edinburgh

prices. Then what happens –
how I do not completely know –
is being stuck in Lockerbie,
that town and also state of mind,

in a rain-swept street
while the young folk
crowd the chip shops and
sing in beautiful raucousness

their plans for love.
My love is not here.
The paving stones and slate
are jet black, gleaming.

Such depths I see in them
and the wash of disappearing
cars and the hard congealing
sky, my land, my life.

The World of Poetry

I saw the poet Donald Adamson
through the window of the World's End.
He was walking on

the wet street and
his head nodded quickly between
the fake cask of sherry on the sill

and a globe on a gold stand.
His small beard shaved Australia.
He lives in Finland and it is rare

for him to be here. It was
one of these chance meetings,
like Ginsberg and Kavanagh

in Greenwich Village in 1963.
I thought briefly of the insights
we could have shared

and how Galloway is a nest
of great words and poets
and then I remembered the

thirty stone Lithuanian I was
sitting with, and the fact
my last bus was in five minutes.

I saw the poet Donald Adamson
through the window of the World's End
and I'm pretty sure he saw me.

Baggage

In the square
is a giant tree
hung with lights.
Through the branches

a blood moon
has come
and gone,
and now

a chain-smoking
player rasps
a wonderful song.
The man next to me

has teeth
dark with wine.
It is about a man
who leaves

his suitcase
in a cupboard,
he says.
Under the tree

an English girl
is weeping,
she has anxieties,
while a step away

a man is
slapping a child

hard on the thigh.
Usually
says my friend
emptying
the bottle,
they are about love.

The Supply Teacher's Last Lesson

Independent variables
are ones you use
to see the effects on
dependent variables,

the ones tested.
Look again at
the PowerPoint
and the worksheets

which have examples
from *Star Wars*
designed especially
to interest you.

No I do not know who
Moff Wilhuff Tarkin is.
Let us imagine
instead that I open

this drawer and there
is a jar of tablets
which I think
could make us fly

from the top of this
1960s tower
vibrating in the wind
like a sore tooth.

I give half of you
the pills and half

of you, the control group,
some sweeties

then we launch off the roof
which is flat concrete,
the odd puddle but
a perfect runway overlooking

the sorry wet fields of our
mothers, the long rows
of houses uniformly grey
apart from those splashed

by emulsion from vigilante groups.
I strain my eyes against
clouds gathering dark as bacon.
Is my hypothesis good?

Are we flying at last,
my broken theories?

Another Push Towards Carlisle

I'm inching towards England
through sidings, rails and yards.
I have been travelling this line
for years and have no idea

about this engineering,
where these tracks go
that fade across the wet lands
like feathers, whether the tower

gleaming in the afternoon light
is state of the art or obsolete.
I only know I go from place to place
each time older, each time

with a sandwich and, of course,
a drink, which makes the view
of the fields more palatable
and has caused a poem or two

to erupt like afternoon gas.
What did Charles Hamilton Sorley say,
yet many a better one has been
written before? That page found

crumpled in his knapsack
will live forever, fresh across
each morning, a twenty year-old's poem,
perfect and ageless. He will not

leave the buffet carriage
and have bad poems dog
his footsteps through days
of bored cows and long shadows.

Confession

Under the tree tonight
is an overweight man
in a garish shirt
who talks incessantly
to his companion
but heartily applauds
every song
even though
he has a cast
on his arm.

Occasionally
the friend puts a hand
solicitously
on his shoulder
as if to calm
or reassure.
There is a book
on the table
in front of them
and the talkative one

is constantly
thumbing it,
turning it over.
I don't hear
the words
but I can tell
he is saying
that he
regrets drinking
so much

and being so gauche
and allowing
obsessions
to interfere
with things
though
he adds in the
same almost
whispered tone
life has such

tragedy sewn
into its fabric
don't you think.
In our beginning
is our end.
The book, I feel,
is exercising
his mind.
It too has a tragic
cover.

The night goes on
and the sea blackens
to the jetty where
lanterns jerk
in the wind.
It is a very
persistent confession
but the man with him
has the endless patience
born
of love.

On the Last Day of my Life

On the last day of my life
I sit three seats down
on the bus as usual
just past the please vacate
this place for a pensioner sign
though I am one really
The driver takes my card
and hands it back with
my ticket – not all do
it is a personal touch
which I appreciate
He is the driver with the stubble
who I joke with sometimes
on the late bus though
I don't know his name
My favourite driver's name
is Robert Louis Stevenson
No joking, he's on the 236

On the last day of my life
I am joined on the bus
by people nicknamed over
the years we've spent this
half hour together
Man-Woman Girders
Good Queen Bess
The Virgin Mary Irish Bob
The Bald Whippet
I've never spoken to them
It is too late for conversations now
but they are often in my mind

through the twists and turns
and all the wet ribbons of road
to Kirkton

On the last day of my life
I go to the carry-out shop
and get a coffee three sweeteners
and two cans of diet Coke
all the gestures to health
that are killing us
In my bag is a ham sandwich
with mustard a variety of pencils
and plastic bags as it is my belief
that when they are in my bag
they are not killing turtles
There is a black
notebook and for a second I am
thinking it is full of bon mots
and half-finished poems
rather than the names of three
legged horses and columns
of diminishing money vanishing
through a single point zero
There is also
a tiny screwdriver I use to
put the lens back in my glasses

On the last day of my life
I am thinking of all the strands
that make up the story
all the impossible clauses
and sub clauses and unlikely
plot developments I am
wondering if those times

my life worked
well with those I love so much
will count for something.
It is Wednesday and starlings
are circling in clouds like atoms
splitting and separating
I am not feeling sorry for myself
merely mentioning all this –
things end
yet simultaneously carry on

A Castle that Might be Stirling

A burst envelope and seventy years
is on the floor, photographs
all sizes, from the box brownie
to the age of instamatic
and earlier: those ones like wafers
too small or dark to make out
but icons you can tell in the story.

Some are flaked, some warped,
but all are unknown to me,
even my own face is unknown to me,
white and swimming up
like in the sea.
Someone with the tiny
beautiful script my family

was famed for should have written –
Boturich 1963, the weather was hot,
the company on edge, behind them
the sun was setting in pieces
by the boathouse –
but my scribes tantalise me
with their hopeless clues,

a name here, a date there
and all that's left is cottages,
smiles for the lost cameraman,
some dahlias, walls,
trees at sunset, a castle
that might be Stirling,
a dog that might be mine.

Reunion

I think of that day in the Palazzo
with crowds off the cruise ships
jostling with other tourists

and the sunlight fragmented through
tile and crenulation, gutter and masts
flashing on tens of thousands

of mobile and tablet screens,
an outpouring of need pointed the way
of the Basilica, its gold leaf ablaze,

and how we made our way as quickly
as possible from that griddle
of humanity past the aims and angles

as if through a firing range.
Now looking back I wonder
how many pictures of the cathedral

have parts of us, perhaps a hand,
a denim collar, a boot, some strands
of hair, a half frown, a quizzical smile,

maybe a hint of that anxiety or hope,
and I wonder if it's possible
on some breakfast bar in Sapporo

or some laptop in Long Beach
or some eternal annexe of the mind
for us to be reassembled again.

Procession

On the harbour road
whose backdrop
is the sea
which I know
is out there
circling promontories
stretching palms
against the shrinking
horizon
a line of small girls
is walking
each holding

a helium balloon
swathed by strings of light
They are different shapes
moons fish unicorns
and these fists of air
float along
gleaming and shivering
against a sky
that for once
has no stars
It is like
a Festival

of the Virgin
but they are
all shrieking
not any song
I know
The lead girl
is Artemis

in a hoodie
she doesn't need
the night is so sultry
Her balloon and
strings are taut

in a sudden wind
It is a procession
marching to the end
of the lit world
it seems to the edge
of darkness
where I know there
is a path I saw it once

between thorn bushes
and rocks
no place
for kids to be

Dream

Midnight and phone dead,
the Innocent Tunnel is a wormhole,
the walls slick and vivid.
I am in Scotland like some vein:
up there all the weans are quiet
and the streets are gaunt and rain
washed and the poets are scheming
and the politicians are sound asleep.

The paths sprout like capillaries.
I take the one that leads to sages,
Tim Propp, Robert Louis Stevenson,
Big Mary of the Songs.
They are talking silently:
there are ruins but no culture, they say,
there is hatred but no criticism.
there are crowds but no community.

Where are our people? the bard asks.
Despite all our most fervent
tweeting we are not saving the world
not even this small part Scotland,
land of glaur and thrawn misery
where the people feast on each other.
We stare at the gas lamps which make
a gauze like glow and the umbers deep

in the well of the bar where we are reflected
over and over again with that beard
or shawl or bicycle receding to infinity.
We sit in mid century silence and

our thoughts turn to those who occupy
our heads like a sullen army. We raise
our tall shining glasses to the dead,
to the list that is unending, to the faces.

I hear my daughter playing a lament:
she has been practising for years
and is now good enough to break my heart.
The tunnel is narrowing into a point
of throat like the foam and then the rest
of a pint might, like being unborn back
into the depths of the atomic soul.
Day will cover the city like a fire blanket.

Here and There

Here I am now
in these braes and shores.
Here is where my mother
walked through snow
to the primary school,

here, another loch side
where she left home.
Here is the doorstep
where her mother and dog
sat in the half light.

Here when all these people
are dead is where
I am, on a rock,
by a loch and while
I am here also,

my daughters
with their upturned
faces fall in love
on pavements that slope
towards the sea.

Getting There

I am going up and down
Scotland like a yo yo
and yes I know I have
been drinking
but words pulse
between water and bark,
clouds round the cold ball
of the sun

and when a heron lazily flaps
to the future
which is over the tree line
or an old man in a pub
holy with dark greens says
that is what my mother

said to me, I feel the
same: as if I have
stumbled on a few
lines that someone
will eventually need to explain.

Storm Glass

After the solar storm of 1859
when the skies of the world
turned lemon, umber and plum
and the North Atlantic boiled

swallowing men and boats,
the government sent
state of the art storm glasses
to fishing villages across

the land with directions
in English and Gaelic.
The glasses were useless
of course – the sea was too

quick even for a skipper's
eye and the rain forecasting
on the roof was more accurate –
but long after the glass

was broken the instructions
could be seen on cottage walls
browning under an official stamp
like small poems or prophecies:

'Mas ann air làithean grianach
a' Gheamhraidh a bhios rionnagan
bìodach san lionn, mar sin a bhios
bochdainn romhainn.'

If the liquid contains tiny stars
on sunny winter days,
then it is certain that
bad times are coming.

Your Day in the Sun

After a year behind
the mirror of the pond,

mayflies rise into the eye
of the sun like a cathedral.

They carry glass green
with light, they dazzle

and shine as the clouds
slowly slide across

the day's face.
It is a parable of grace

and patience,
it is a story of the heart,

so intricately worked,
dispelled in air.

That is the Way that Time Works

The shadow of a bird passes,
clouds break and blot.
I carry my mind from chair

to chair – it is a Droz clock,
levers and lights
and scenes in silhouette,

it is unstoppable it thinks,
dipping into the past
like a swan. This happened,

that happened:
it thinks we are enthralled.
Smell of cut grass

and rain,
getting up for the door.
That is the way that time works.

With their Violins

Lydia has gone,
her face carefully made up.
She had her rucksack,

suitcase, and violin.
Here the blackbird sings loudly
and would, even if Lydia

hadn't gone: it is a music
that is irrepressible.
Somewhere Lydia will

get her violin restrung
and begin again that
life that is hers. It is not easy

to contemplate this but
we all have our parts to play,
it is like a conspiracy

or game. These girls
walking away with violins
against a dazzling

sleeve of sky,
it is the most inspiring
and saddest thing.

Ghosts of the Scaur

I

Each day I try to walk
a path that isn't shown,
but is underfoot delicate
as a vein below the skin
of soil and mould.

They lead to fords
and crossings, styles,
stones slung haphazardly
across glassy streams.
Sometimes there

are bridges
and no rivers, as if the land
has slipped like a rug
beneath our shoes and

rivers somehow
became burns
and burns somehow
became scars in the earth.
There are no maps,

but in the mind
at the crossing point
of day and night,
it is easy to see
my brothers and sisters,
the traders, the soldiers,

the travellers, the drovers,
the pilgrims, the poets,
shouldering their packs,
walking forever
in the woods.

2

Across the night
horned by cold
one owl then another

in eery harmony.
We flit from one topic
to the next,

love and hate, talk
money, plot in
alleyways,

fall apart and die,
and during all that,
owls phrase

songs with such
precision
that the stars

turn out to
light the
hapless world.

3

I walked along rutted
tractor footprints
and puddles hard as pearl

to a loch on top of the world,
a silver scar in a basin
of felled pine,

a single teardrop,
an eye open to heaven
below a ball of cloud.

I asked what there is to say
now the world is done.
A heron spoke, or the wind

through gaps in dykes.
Keep asking, it said, always ask:
not a word is wasted.

Chronicles of Rain

This bit of drizzle or smirr
is part of the great union
of rain, affiliated to the
consolidated bodies of water.

It has no rainbow
or sheen to recommend it,
just a plug ugly droplet
oiling down the window pane

but it will one day join the Gulf
of Carpentaria or the Great Bear,
and be part of the legends
and stories that they tell

there of the world starting
with a single drop of rain.
It will be the pips in the lotus
and the green fuse of the Acheron.

How I admire the rain,
its way of sitting unashamed
in the puddles,
knowing this is not the end.

A Breath

I watch a small boy go to school:
the trees are thickening

and the sun is a little lemon
slice of almost Spring.

It is a short way between
the Keir Road and the church lane,

about four feet of windowpane
and a minute till the school bell.

While I reach for my toast
he is hopscotching the white lines,

while I pick it up
he is skipping to the litter bin,

while I open my mouth
he is squeezing between the bin

and the wall -an impossible feat-
while I am closing my lips

he has run around the
plant tub, and parkoured

the bus stop bench. I have not
begun to taste the toast,

and my day is almost over.
Time is not unbending

for him, he crosses
the sky like a breath.

A Casual Conversation

I didn't like you much,
and I know it was mutual,
and our conversation
in that beer garden

was banal,
but nonetheless we had it,
and it was your last,
and I have so many questions

now I would value the time
to chat, like when it was,
on that summer evening,
you decided to die,

and whether it was a slow
sinking like water tipping
over bulkheads,
or a sudden blast like light.

Was it accompanied
by a sign or just birdsong
muting in your head,
did some ennui spread

and darken and fill
your veins so it seemed
the most natural thing to
disconnect and go?

So much to talk about:
the fact is I feel
closer to you
than ever before.

Two Men Below a Bad Weather Forecast

While a storm is
circling Scotland
two men

drink
There are hot springs
in Iceland

and crystal
coves in Greece
and bubbles

in the wallpaper
Is that sudden glare
light refracted

through harmless
particles of air
-remember

when air was-
or something else
It's certain

that fourteen
pints is bad but
under the circumstances

Pestes

Public Safety Advice Oan the Brent-New Pestilence 1348

If ye hae been fair awa
or hae met onyane traivellin
frae a kennt hot-spot
ie Asia Minor, the Crimea,
Genoa not Venice
an ye begin tae shaw
the followin signs:

Myld filever,
spreckle-lik spots,
pechin,
byles in the oxters

an if it isnae possible locally
tae thraw a jew
or a humphy-backit wummin
doon a well, dinnae fash –

adopt the following meesures:

buy or mak a mask wi a big beak
an bide cosy in yer hoose!
There is nae evidence
the disease spreids tae pets
sae dinnae fret aboot yer rottans,
looses, golachs, sclaturs
or mites they will be jist braw.

Bounty

I smell wild garlic and crushed
grass. I am glad of that,
for a symptom of the disease

they say is to lose that hold
on life, another treasure
gone, like breath.

We are safe here, though
the river talks all the time,
not always reassuringly.

After the wind,
the water carries away
leaf and tree blossom,

in a time of stasis
we turn to old exports.
I name this broken branch

the 'Bountiful Blessing of Scaur',
it is a two-master, a caravel.
Here world, our fruit,

the stuff that in lockdown
we have been making
in our fabulous groves,

with no machine in sight.
Anemones in their crowded
docks wave like hankies,

birds sing your anthems
to pipe our cargoes
on their heavy way to sea.

Two Worlds

I follow my eyes to the hills
and the swallows spelling words
in the air. No more than
twenty miles that way
is the sea: we are in a sleeve

of land between two worlds.
Here it is Spring. The girls move
easily through the woods,
they were born in this well of light,
but at night we watch a digger

shoving the cheap coffins
of the countless dead
into a builder's trench, the poor,
the dispossessed, the loveless.
Drone high in a dank New York

afternoon, we are staring
once more down the cuff
of history to the bone beneath.
Eritrea, Darfur, Elmhurst Hospital.
A tide of negligence and cruelty

too high and ageless to resist.
We switch the TV off, drink tea.
Tomorrow the anemone will shine
like tiny stars. The birds have always
sung at Auschwitz.

Flattening the Curve

Bombarded daily by
poets, topiarists, cake decorators,
cartoonists, expressive dancers,
all committed to seeing us

through this toughest of times,
I am reminded of the fact
that out of the babies enrolled
in the very first creative immersion
project in America in the 1960s,
ten percent became serial killers.

The Ballad of Bessie Bell and Mary Gray

Bessie Bell and Mary Gray
isolated by the Burn Brae.
They were the most beautiful
girls in Scotland they say,
their faces held the luminosity
of the sun on fresh grass
but they had eyes only
for each other, theirs was
a passion rich and very diverse
for a 17th century ballad.

Their groceries were left
at the loan-end by the local
shop and the girls would
spend the afternoon washing
the tins of tuna and packets
of potato scones in the stream
which that spring flowed
clear and sweet from hills,
till but recently hooded in snow.
It was a season of rare

light and heat and birdsong
and periodically they would
skype their fathers for news.
Their weakness was poetry
however and because some
teacher had once told them girls
couldn't write any, an itinerant
poet was drawn, with his man-bag

and bunnet, to their lustre
as though to fire, and came
every evening to recite
his tawdry verses and creep
closer and closer to the rush-
strewn bothy. Because he had
a big twitter following
and a book out soon (he said)
from some Indie publisher
in Edinburgh they did not
shoot him with the Black Bess
they kept for water fowling

but gave in instead to entreaties
to receive his pamphlet,
the font and pagination
of which were award nominated
and a delight to the eye.
And that was that.
The grass grew over the graves
of Bessie Bell and Mary Gray,
the blackbirds sang, and the poet
never got further than a small

residency, even with this powerful
new material. But through
the ballads we still remember
them, their lips locked in love,
their hair crowned in light,
their potent and efficacious
message, that poetry
is an infectious and ultimately
fatal disease, resonant still
to this very day.

Three Days in May

On the hottest day in May
my daughter found
a barely feathered bird,

rescued it from under
the gaze of a neighbour's cat,
cradled it back,

homed it in a shoe box
not far from the pile of
books sorted for uni

lording it on
the bedroom floor.
A half-way house

in a half-way house,
between Phase Two
and Phase Three,

a lockdown bird,
scruffy yellow and needy
requiring all the care

the internet could give,
a bit of boiled egg, hard
cat food dampened down.

She set her alarm clock
to feed it, speculated
what would happen when

it began to fly, how we'd cope.
They have their own
radar their own instincts

what a joy to see them
navigate the steps of sky.
For three whole days

this thrill hung in stasis
like the air itself, heavy
with perfume.
On the fourth morning the bird
was dead. Who knows why,
another mystery to add

to all the others.
We buried it below dianthus,
her sister ringed the grave

with white stones.
A season shut but still opening.
She went back to pack.

It's not Sunday it's Tuesday

The burn knows no days:
sometimes it bubbles with rain
other times it shrugs slowly
through the neck of grass like some
teenager who's slept till three.

When someone cycles
past I've never seen before,
it's a moment. Where did
she come from, that one?
Some gap between worlds

she has slipped through,
Thornhill or Madagascar.
It will soon be the time for lambs
to be separated from ewes
and the glen will be filled

with weeping. Such sadness
does not rely on calendars
really but the cruelty of the sun
as we turn around.
I sit here in the glen

on this flat stone
and I can swear I am rooted
here like in some myth,
staring into the days,
as my stars leave the sky.

Book in the Grass

I dream in poems now
tomorrow is for the woken up –
bars in Stockholm beaches in Australia –
these images come in daily
they are part
of another world
Here it is merciless
Birdsong a vapour trail from
some military jet
clouds forming reforming
making continents
extinct animals
Up the stairs the kids
will sleep this off
#lockdown20 remember?
a stumble on the step
Myself I am the Russian
on that book cover on the grass
half hidden waiting for the day
to end

Keep Smiling Through

It is no coincidence that
the VE celebrations
coincide with Britain's
epic victory over coronavirus.

Deck the halls with bunting
and wear the face mask
free in the Virus-Bashing
Souvenir Edition of the *Daily Mail*

for the sun is shining at last
in the uplands. Your sacrifice
has again brought us victory.
It is not over of course

there is a long way to go:
remember to swallow
the narrative
three times a day

for it was not the Russians
or the Indians in Burma
who won the war
but our plucky pensioners –

not the dead ducks
in social care of course,
but the ones marching
down long and dreamy

gardens with zimmers
while above Spitfires

salute lazily over
hop fields combed

by specially imported
Rumanians shipped here
by Amazon. In the reheated
words of the forces sweetheart,

not the squeaky one with
the dodgy private life,
but the posh sounding one,
keep smiling through.

All This Time

In the woods
where I roam, the Glen
between the two rivers,
young horses run

when the throat of the sky
closes and night comes.
I had been imagining
all these weeks

I was alone here –
my weans at home
bathed in screen-light,
my kind shuttered up

stowed against the news
that rips across the slates
like sea – but suddenly
I find I am not:

a dyker has been working,
slowly packing the walls
that cross land and
years like old sentences,

tight, elegant, other-worldly.
He has been so slow
I had not noticed, but yet
look at him now so far

away on the brow of a hill
that he is merging with cloud.

This quite ordinary man,
this engineer, this bookbinder,

this clock fixer,
this shaman, all this time
he has been
mending the seams.

Caravan

The south wind is here
moving on the river like sandals.

Tall trees bend, blossom
is gossip on water. This wind

was in deserts earlier
and carries salt and sand,

the heat of dreams. It has
moved among the dying.

It says in the north we are not
so different: our eagles

stand on air, we too
walk between worlds.

Positioning Three Words in a Poem

While the broadband is being
strummed by all the air guitarists
I am sitting among the flowers
considering the positioning
of three words in a poem.

I am positioning three words in a poem
while blackbirds leave
questions in the air
and Brian the cat next door
turns blank eyes to the cloudless sky.

The positioning of three words in a poem
is not hard work or work at all really,
it is like imagining
three drops of water on a leaf,
any order would do, or any leaf.

I think positioning three words in a poem
on this day pretending
to be summer
is like a renaissance painting,
the hermit crouched over

his gnomic text
while through the window behind
the whole world
writhes in a dazzle
of war or plague.

Or in fact maybe
it is like opening the mind

with three perfectly milled
keys so I see the Argolid
or Angourie,

the light on the sea smoking
between the pines,
and that somehow enters
the poem too and infuses
each word I am positioning

with a different meaning
so a new poem builds
up marvellously around them
like scaffolding in the sun.
And that poem speaks

as all do of love.
I am confident that these
three very ordinary words
I am positioning in this poem
are now sacred words

in the order I imagined them,
or any other,
and I will leave them here
on the grass for now,
in this circle of light.

Sources

I am walking alone
along the banks of the river
where under a pale bridge
the Shinnel meets the Scaur.

It is Spring and the land
is lucky, it is effortlessly
recoding, beginning again
with fresh tree blossom

that is sweet to smell.
It is different for us.
Though I will not get there today,
I am moving towards the ocean,

past green pools,
our scratchings in the soil,
broken walls and branches,
babble, love and strife,

my children haunting
the verges their faces
round as moons. Everything
will pass down the Nith,

through the Solway even,
until all the dazzle of stuff
that's made me is lost in the
dreaming heart of the sea.

The Cyanometer

Among the cargo of special
scientific instruments
on the Pizarro for
Alexander Von Humboldt's

expedition to Cuba,
someone stashed a cyanometer,
and when the ship was laid up
in Venezuela by epidemic

Humboldt spent quarantine
staring down this instrument
at the eye of the sky and its
fifty-three dazzling veins of blue.

Soon afterwards he learned
Aturian from a parrot,
watched a meteor shower
and climbed a mountain

with Simon Bolivar's
favourite poet.
I'm not saying that was a result:
it could have happened anyway.

The New Old Age

I am looking at the contents
of my coat pocket:
a train ticket, a pencil
plucked from the playground,
a receipt for a steak pie

and large glass
of Sauvignon blanc,
and I think I should put
these on a shelf as symbols
of a lost and easy age

of innocence.
It is enough almost
to make you weep
this sacred detritus,
rubbish pregnant now

with such meaning.
When we emerge
blinking into the future
with our long hair,
our chipped teeth,

our bandaged specs,
will those months
of self-help, yoga,
soda bread and scrabble
swell our brains

to the size of a new world?
Will poetry have seen us through?
I think, jealous
of their high-fiving freedom
through our long days

of want and envy,
we will swarm out to find a rook
to strangle while nature
scatters with a collective sigh
of here's this lot on the piss again.

Next Year

Pressed
against glass
we see birds
form fantastic
prophecies.

They are dreaming
but next year
we will hog
the air again.
Next year

is like a hill
just beyond
the limit
of the daily walk
It is like a painting

we have shared
from lockdown
to ease ourselves
and others'
mental health.

It is like
an enamel,
a poem,
a Chinese miniature,
it is guarded

now by animals
and fabulous
with snow
but we will make
short work of it.

Carol

*'In that bed there lieth a knight
His woundes bleeding day and night
By his side there kneeleth a may
And she weepeth night and day.
Lully lullay, lully lullay.'*

We have modelled the Milky Way,
and grafted DNA like creeper.
We have antidote. Science
has restored our swagger,
all the killers and lovers.

Written already as last year's
story are endless days
of blossom, the ink of river
and sky, strange embassies:
a stag, a hawk, a weasel, a fox.

I wonder what grace
we still possess. My child
has the eyes of a doe;
the world bleeds
in its bower in the woods.

Birthday 2021

There's a blunt wind, sunlight
is favouring some clouds,
trees are leafing up,

a bright orange digger
sits in a field stubbled with
stalks, a jackdaw

lies dead in the grass
near the pylon, gleaming black.
My phone offers

to sell me pictures in a book,
all my birthdays
bubbles in one stream.

I am walking
past a dyke that's spilled
open, there's a hole

to the sky. I make no great
claims: I am 8.6 kilometres
away from yesterday.

Prospects

Poem on a bus ticket

I've only a bus ticket to write on
but luckily it's a Houston's Bus ticket
which has one whole side blank
and is bigger than most others.
Only a bus ticket but I have a feverish
need to fill it with poetry. No room
to rage at the world's injustices
or how hard fulfilment is, or the sadness
of looking back, only enough space
to salute the sun which is filling the last
blank corner of this bus ticket
with a wild and supernatural blazing.

The Path below the Linden Tree

The moon shimmers,
mercury on the tips of trees,
their flowers like stars on earth.
Never such silence:

no traffic no music no chat
just a path of light
from the sky and the
perfume of the lindens

so strong, so evocative
of something in the past,
sweet just beyond touching.
Follow the path to where

it ritually goes,
old gardens, wild woods,
the brain, the soul,
wherever. It's the road home.

A Thursday Morning in May

A Thursday morning in May,
the town swept by fine rain

and through this frame of a window
people move unabashed, wonderfully:

a red-faced man hawks in the gutter,
two hearty school girls meet

and exchange blasphemies,
toddlers stomp on the wet stone

and the slight rheumy beginnings
of puddles. Here's a hairdresser

with a lunchbox,
two women sculpted like Nefertiti,

an old lady moving towards
the locked door of the Loreburn Centre.

Dumfries as ever is bending at a crazy angle
from here over a hill to history,

tipping its gentle morning folk
through all their bewildering doors.

Nigel and Kenny

Nigel and Kenny
are playing tonight
at the mouth of the black void
that is the Aegean.

Out there is a worrying
absence of anything:
it is a wound scoured
by the imagination

nightly: the boats
full of children thrown
like corks,
acrid seas on burning coasts.

Here though Nigel and Kenny
are keeping the night
and the creeping realisation
of death at bay

by playing cover versions
of seventies classics.
Huge men in shorts
dance. Like reanimated

corpses,
they jerk and shine.
Get it on, bang a gong, get it on
Get it on, bang a gong, get it on.

Couple, New Cumnock

He's drinking strawberry hooch
and adding to it
from a green vial
like in a horror film,

she is half sleeping on her
handbag. They both look
about fifteen but my compass
is off on these matters.

The train is passing
New Cumnock, and he takes
his parka off to cover her,
even though she already

has a parka, and strokes
her face under a curl
of blonde hair
that seems carelessly

arranged but has taken
a hundred thousand years
of human evolution
to place in exactly that

heartbreaking manner
on her white cheek.
I want to say cherish
and take care,

but somehow it's like
a painting and I wouldn't

say cherish and take care
to a masterpiece

even a flawed one,
so I watch them instead
poised like this
while the rain comes down.

Advice to the Makars
Wigtown 2019

I am talking of Willie Neill
here where the echoes
of the bards are clasped

in names like feldspar.
The MacNellie, the Filidh,
the Neill, wrote the verses

that defined a country
which seems so much the same
but altered utterly.

For those of whatever tongue
who stand astride our past
and what's to come,

learn all the stories:
then for you the birds
will hang in air

the sea will breathe and shine
and the poems
will be waiting to be written.

t reynolds

There is a stone here,
no embellishments just t reynolds
carved in economical
lower case script like water main

or triangulation point. There is a small
gap between t and reynolds,
not enough to encourage
speculation. It has fallen at an angle

away from the other graves
and lies against the verge
so t reynolds is the first thing
people see in this ramshackle

place. When they walk their dogs
or snog below the broken wall
t reynolds will be there quietly in the
back of their minds, when bikers

use him as a ramp his name will be
a small runway to the stars.
This is the role of the unassuming
in the memory of the world

though he would not see it like this.
His final letter to us
had no dreams or wild predictions,
just t reynolds.

Licht

It's a we want.
Scotland's aye dooked in mire.
Fur guid.

Mair than hauf the year
we keek oot
an the laund is deid

dreich meets dreich
in a clamjamfry o dreich.
In a wee chink

o summer, yons
the time for it:
some grand lassie
to lead us oot o glaur.

Sunday

Mid Ayrshire sun
turns to South Ayrshire
fatigue grey
A man stands solitary in a loch
tiny trees stretch like a savannah
past broken dykes
and beyond to a krall of tile
and pebble dash New Cumnock

Earlier the water of Leith
was chlorophyll green
wild flowers in clouds
and last night there was
poetry and music
beneath a bare bulb
a conversation in Cantonese
Life seems random things

like tape spliced
and the only thing
connecting the bulb
the trees the man
the flowers those words
thrown haphazardly
in the starless night
is me

My worlds
my words my miracles

A Break in the Weather

I met the under-18s
European Girls' Ice Hockey
Champions on a traffic island
tonight: it was that

one on the corner
of Buccleuch St
where the crossing takes
ages, hours can pass.

They spent the
time savagely thumping each
other on the shoulders
and singing a song

by Selena Gomez.
Each one was giant
and raucous
and wore a padded anorak

emblazoned with
a jagged lightning bolt.
Thin passers by gawped,
shrivelled into wet doorways

to watch. Such a stunning
crew was never assembled
on any traffic island
in history.

I was expecting a slow
walk through puddled streets

as always,
lukewarm drizzle,

buses, rain-pocked
streetlamps,
but instead Dumfries
stood on its ear

as if a keel had grounded
on the old shale
of the Whitesands
and landed life.

From Here to the Sea

I have flushed out animals today:
a young deer bolting across
wet grass near Kilmaurs
and a hawk at Garelochhead
arrowing between trees.

Maybe it was the train did it,
but I think it was me nosing north
like the hawk on a wing and a prayer,
like the deer on a body swerve.
Sunlight is strung through cloud

and ahead the weather is bending
like a bar round mountains.
This is as ever a journey
from the central belt of my life
to the hills of my imagination,

hard to describe:
sometimes I run beside the train,
sometimes the dead live,
their conversation
frozen in solid ice.

The country is alive too –
the rocks breathe and even
the rain is saying something
dripping in a romance language
down wet windows.

Oh a heron! Sheet music
beating from here to the sea.

Relocation Relocation

In the midst of a gyre of leaves,
autumn red rags carrying our sad
messages to the skies and brushing

ancient windows as they go, I am
watching on the TV two youngsters
in Australia looking for a house,

and there is literally a huge yard
in Queensland where all the unwanted
houses go and you can turn up

and buy one and take it where
you want by truck. What a great thing
that is: no mouldering in damp or

getting cleared by needy children
or being turned into AirBnBs
so that folk can come and imagine the history

they've helped to kill. Time to cast off
the thrall of heritage and simply begin again,
a series of wonderful new starts.

I want this place next time
at the seaside, no kids, maybe an
eccentric couple of ladies who read

detective novels and enjoy finding things
on the beach. I'd like the house
to smell very strongly of dog.

Showers may clear away from the Dalmuir area this afternoon

A blade of sunlight rips through
the train like an electric current
and suddenly in a riot of movement
they are tearing off their puttees

and shawls and the sandals they've cut
from the tires of old Renault Clios.
Chickens and goats run free,
towers of Helensburgh cheese

dip and sway, girls expose their shoulders
which tan miraculously, porpoises leap
in the sea glittering like gentian.
Poverty and injustice

are no longer guddles mired in talk
but stark, assailable, like peaks emerging
from cloud and darkness.
People of Drumry, Rekindle your fire!

Consign the dull grind of stupidity
to a place in the mind with weather
forecasts and 10 in a row. Join your
children in making hats from pages

of the Daily Record, pulped
and dyed with Alconia berries
bright as blood. Teeter them
on your golden, peasant heads!

Crossing the Spheres

In this saucer of cloud
and mulch, the wise
trees have stopped talking,
the kids are going mental,

and at each clock turn
I hear my mother's words
as she stared up a road
stricken with rain – aye,

another day nearer death.
I am tired of doing things
that humans do, even
compiling that list of folk

I hate that brought me such
comfort in Spring. All thought
is just an excuse for more:
an endless procession

of tired salesmen, jugglers
and born again maniacs.
Where did it all go wrong?
Sometime between the release

of *Songs of Love and Hate*
and David Narey's goal
against Brazil maybe, some
afternoon that turned

to rain. Listen. The geese
are hurdling the spheres.
Give me half a goose brain
and aim me for wide water.

Long View

The train draws
out of Fort William
and slowly passes
the Primary
and a wee fellow
with an overlong

jumper and bright
red cheeks has jumped
on a stump to wave
and has been
doing this
since 1895

when the railway
came and
before that
the mail coach
and before that
the greylag goose.

No one is
on my train
cos the world is
in a dazzle of fear
and stasis but that
wee boy's waving

and waving
and all his mates
are shaking their heads
as though he's daft
but he's got
the long view.

Carbonation

A young man is talking
to a girl about carbonation.
He is French I think,
she might be Spanish, I'm not sure.

They have a common
language, carbonation,
and have been talking about it
from Glasgow to Ardlui.

He has been carbonating
for a few years and it is a tricky
technique. They are pressed
close, but in a liquid way,

changing shape as the tube
of the train lurches
through rain. Her hair is black
on his shoulder and he talks

into her glistening ear,
a hand on her waist, the short
floral skirt. At one point during
the conversation she climbs

onto his lap the better
to talk about carbonation.
The heady mix of different
elements at boiling point,

the pressure to contain.
I have never properly
understood the process
of carbonation till now.

Holy Lemon You

The river is fast after rain
but the sun is hanging out
as if it's June.
Break open a bottle

of shine while the nymphs
and selkies washed here
waft in pools, stones
glittering in their teeth.

Cast our backpacks
with their breaded fish
and beetroot aside
and dance on the brink:

the peewits will be
amazed at our insouciance.
Spread me your jewels
unconquerable sun,

infuse these grass tips,
warm up this pen,
the summer we write
will be full of poems:

this is what we live for,
this palm of moment,
reaching out to squeeze
like a fruit, holy lemon you.

I am No Mariner

Let me describe
the thrill in the wake
of the boat
when light sparks
as though part
of the sun has fused,

so the sky is plunged
into jagged dark,
and we fumble
between islands
till one arrives,
where we hope we

can dock and not
get turned away.
My stomach is
somewhere off
Sull Ghorm circling
in a well of water,

my eyes are straining
like birds,
but I keep moving,
though I am
no mariner,
no mariner at all.

I am here because
the sun and sea
make a map of me.
It is the writing
of these journeys
not the arriving.

Are We There Yet?

A dark sea lit by stars.
A crescent bends an ear
to the distance, the echo of
waves on shale and rock.
It is the sound of the west.
Seabirds take us home.

Acknowledgements

Some of these poems first appeared in *The Rialto*, *New Writing Scotland*, *The Glasgow Review*, *Backstory*, *Stilts*, *The North*, *Takahe*, *Poetry Review*, *Raceme*, *Acumen*, *Agenda*, *The Blue Bottle Journal*, *Noble Gas Quarterly*, *Creative Flight Journal*, *Northwords*, and the pamphlets *Dodeka* and *The Blash o God*. 'The New Old Age' was commissioned for *Scotland After the Virus* (Luath Press, ed. Gerry Hassan and Simon Barrow) and 'Dream' by the Scottish Poetry Library as part of the 2020 'Poetry Champions' project. 'The Alexandria Quartet' first appeared in *The Other Creatures in the Wood* published by Mariscat Press.

Luath Press Limited

committed to publishing well written books worth reading

LUATH PRESS takes its name from Robert Burns, whose little collie Luath (*Gael.*, swift or nimble) tripped up Jean Armour at a wedding and gave him the chance to speak to the woman who was to be his wife and the abiding love of his life. Burns called one of the 'Twa Dogs' Luath after Cuchullin's hunting dog in Ossian's *Fingal*. Luath Press was established in 1981 in the heart of Burns country, and is now based a few steps up the road from Burns' first lodgings on Edinburgh's Royal Mile. Luath offers you distinctive writing with a hint of unexpected pleasures.

Most bookshops in the UK, the US, Canada, Australia, New Zealand and parts of Europe, either carry our books in stock or can order them for you. To order direct from us, please send a £sterling cheque, postal order, international money order or your credit card details (number, address of cardholder and expiry date) to us at the address below. Please add post and packing as follows: UK – £1.00 per delivery address; overseas surface mail – £2.50 per delivery address; overseas airmail – £3.50 for the first book to each delivery address, plus £1.00 for each additional book by airmail to the same address. If your order is a gift, we will happily enclose your card or message at no extra charge.

Luath Press Limited
543/2 Castlehill
The Royal Mile
Edinburgh EH1 2ND
Scotland
Telephone: +44 (0)131 225 4326 (24 hours)
Email: sales@luath.co.uk
Website: www.luath.co.uk